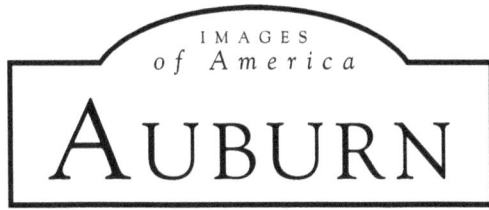

IMAGES
of America

AUBURN

This stairway led from the back of the Washburn School, through the "gully," to the AAA Park.

IMAGES
of America

AUBURN

Bonnie Pierpont

ARCADIA
PUBLISHING

Published by Arcadia Publishing
Charleston, South Carolina

Library of Congress Catalog Card Number: 2009931263

For all general information contact Arcadia Publishing at:
Telephone 843-853-2070
Fax 843-853-0044
E-mail sales@arcadiapublishing.com
For customer service and orders:
Toll-Free 1-888-313-2665

Visit us on the Internet at www.arcadiapublishing.com

A view of Auburn taken from Goff Hill.

Contents

Introduction

Auburn and Lewiston are considered sister cities; known as the "Twin Cities," they share a heritage and history on opposite sides of the Androscoggin River. The first settlers were drawn to the area by the "falls," lakes, and streams, including what we now call Lake Auburn and Taylor Pond. They built their homes and mills along the waterways, and in such choice locations as Goff's Corner, Stevens Mills, Danville, West Auburn, and North Auburn. The Androscoggin River provided power for early shoe and textile manufacturers in both Lewiston and Auburn, from the pre-Civil War era until well into the twentieth century. The waterways also provided opportunities for recreation, and in the nineteenth century tourism boomed, with people "from away" flocking to enjoy cruises on Lake Auburn aboard the steamer *Lewiston*, and to partake of "spring water" and "tonic."

According to local lore, Mrs. James Goff, when asked to select a name for the early town, chose a name from Oliver Goldsmith's poem, *The Desert Village*: "Sweet Auburn, loveliest village of the plain." Auburn extends approximately 12 miles along the Androscoggin River and covers an area of about 50 square miles; one-sixth of that is water, and includes one-half of the original town of Minot, and also Danville (originally called Pejepscot). Lake Auburn, formerly Wilson Pond, is approximately 4 miles long and about 2 miles wide at its broadest point, and today is a source of public water for the area.

Photographers, whether they knew it at the time or not, have done an excellent job documenting the last 130 years of Auburn's past. Through their lenses we can see the houses of old, the modes of dress, the places where people worked and went to school, and moments of leisure. They also photographed disasters, such as the Great Flood of 1896, and the many celebrations and parades that brought the community together. Many of the people, places, and homes are no longer around, but the photographs enable us to "keep them alive." Perhaps you will find the name of an ancestor, relative, or friend in the many classroom pictures throughout the book. Enjoy!

One

People and Pets

William Miller and steed were photographed in this view looking up Goff Hill.

William P. Frye was born in Lewiston in 1831, and graduated from Bowdoin College. He was the state attorney general from 1867 to 1869 and was also a U.S. Senator until he resigned in 1881.

This horse was named "Linus," which is Latin for "flaxed-haired." It had a beautifully-groomed mane and tail, and was photographed at the Island Garden, an entertainment center located between Lewiston and Auburn. The horse's mane was 14 feet 8 inches in length, and its tail was 12 feet 3 inches long. It was owned by C.H and H.W. Eaton.

This group of Auburn "corn roasters" was captured on film in 1889.

The Auburn "corn roasters" were "founded" in August 1866 by Sewall C. Parker, who decided to take his dinner in the open air. He ventured forth to "Pettengill Gully," started a small fire, and prepared his dinner, which consisted of "corn in milk," eggs, coffee, and other "fixins." After roasting his corn, he communed with nature, and had such a good time that he repeated

oasters 1900

the event in the same manner in 1867, along with his brother Charles. In 1868, the third annual outing was enjoyed by Sewall, Charles, and James Parker, all brothers. The group slowly grew in numbers and the tradition continued.

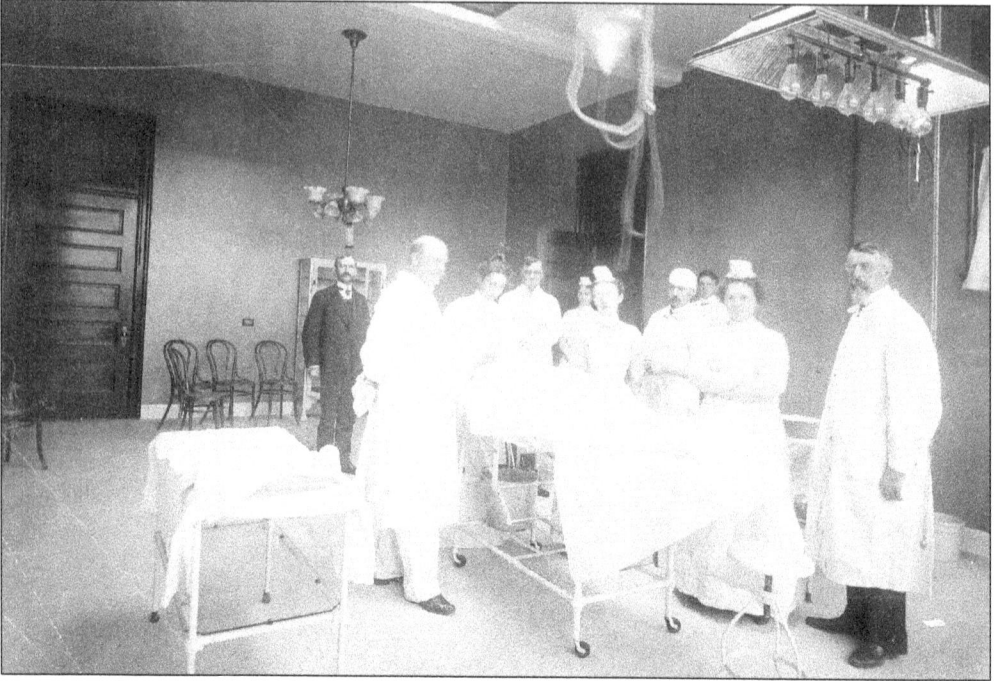

Doctors and nurses stand ready to receive a patient in the operating room at the Central Maine General Hospital.

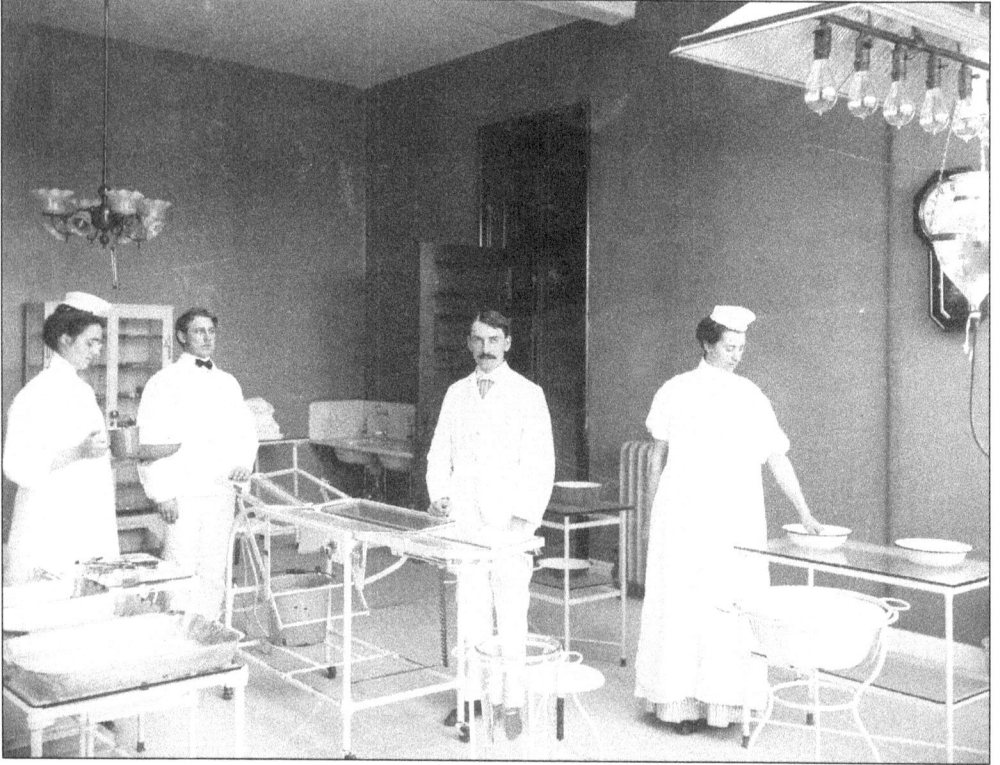

This early photograph shows doctors and nurses in the operating room.

A nurse waits on a patient in a private hospital room.

Miss Lamberson and Miss R. Metcalf posed at the Central Maine General Hospital in 1912.

On "Grand Army Field Day," members of the "Mary Cotton Tent, D.U.V." and officers and guests of the "Custer Post" gathered at the home of Mr. and Mrs. Henry

Glidden on upper Turner Street.

Eben D. Jordan, an Auburn resident and founder of the Jordan Marsh Company of Boston, posed for this photograph with Mrs. Julia Jordan (his wife) and his children: Eben Jr., James, and Julia.

These doctors lived in Lewiston and Auburn and were affiliated with the Central Maine General Hospital. Included in this *c.* 1910 photograph are: Dr. B.F. Sturgis (front row, second from left), Dr. Philoon (front row, third from right), Dr. Dixon (front row, second from right), Dr. Williams (front row, far right), Dr. Webber (middle row, fourth from left), Dr. Call (middle row, fifth from left), Dr. Cobb (middle row, sixth from left), Dr. Dan Barrell (back row, third from left), and Dr. Walter Pennell (back row, fourth from right).

F.W. Adams owned a hardware store and lumber yard, located on Turner Street.

Ansel Briggs, son of Hiram, was a long-time resident of Auburn.

Lewiston and Auburn's Marketmens' Association on their seventh annual excursion with their ladies to Fort Popham and the islands of Boothbay Harbor. Glover's Band from Auburn accompanied the group on August 23, 1882, and is seated to the right.

Amos Fitz, of Fitz Bros., looks quite regal in this photograph. Fitz Bros. owned a "last" factory (a 'last" was a form around which a shoe was made).

James Monroe was the owner of James Munroe & Co., which began as Packard and Monroe in 1843. The company closed in 1880, after operating continuously for thirty years, with the exception of two months in 1861 during preparations for the Civil War.

Joshua Freeman is shown here hoeing the cabbages in his Orr's Island garden. His grandson, Freeman Robinson, wore his grandfather's hat during the Auburn Centennial Celebration and won a prize. The hat and other clothing of Joshua Robinson were donated to the Androscoggin Historical Society.

Nelson Dingley Jr., the eldest son of Nelson and Jane L. Dingley, was born in Durham, Maine, on February 15, 1832. He was a good student and enrolled in Waterville College (now Colby College) in 1851, and after a one-and-a-half-year stint, he transferred to Dartmouth College to continue his studies, graduating in 1855. Mr. Dingley studied law with Morrill and Fessenden in Auburn and in 1856 was admitted to the bar. He chose to enter the field of journalism rather than practice law and in September 1856 purchased one-half interest in the *Lewiston Journal*. A year later he became the full owner and editor of the same. Mr. Dingley was elected to represent Auburn in the Maine Legislature and was elected speaker of the house during the 1863 session. His career in politics continued and in 1873 he was elected governor of Maine as a Republican. In 1881, Governor Dingley was elected to the U.S. Congress to fill a vacancy caused by the resignation of William P. Frye.

Mayor Nathan Harris and the Auburn City Government gathered for a *c.* 1895 portrait.

This is a 1918 photograph of the first Red Cross volunteers of Auburn and Lewiston. From left to right are: (front row) Miss Annia Wiseman, Mrs. C.W. Lawlor, Miss Hazel Mitchell, Miss Annia Brawshaw, Mrs. Iva Safford, Mrs. F.H. Packard, Mrs. C.C. Peaslee, Mrs. Hattie Allen, and Miss Therma Hicks; (back row) Mrs. Charles Bosehby, Mrs. Ashely Thurston, Mrs. Merton Warren, Mrs. John McMurrey, Mrs. F.A. Jones, Miss Lorena A. Chaplin, Mrs. A.W. Auehowy, and Miss Helen McCaretry.

Horatio Foss co-founded Dingley, Foss, & Co., which manufactured opera boots and slippers as well as a line of sporting goods. The business began operating in 1856 at 5 Roak Block, and employed seventy-five to eighty people during its first year of operation. The company was later moved to Railroad Square.

Judge John Adams Morrill was born in Auburn on June 23, 1855. The son of Nahum and Anne Isabelle Morrill, he graduated from Bowdoin College and in 1918 was named associate justice of the Supreme Court.

Judge Harry Manser of Auburn was appointed to the Superior Court bench in 1928, succeeding Justice Henry W. Oaks. Judge Manser was born in England on April 20, 1874, and died on February 20, 1955. He was active in community affairs, including service as, but not limited to, vice-president of the state Y.M.C.A., president of Auburn Savings Bank, and trustee of the Auburn Home for Aged Woman.

Photography subjects were not limited to the human species, as evidenced by a local kitty cat posing in a bucket.

George Pearl Martin worked at the Crest Shoe and Leather Bank.

Two

Veterans

This photograph of Company C of the Auburn Light Infantry was taken on May 2, 1898. The Russ Bradbury Livery Stable is on the banks of the river on the left. It would later be the place of business of "Libby and Pettingill," followed by the First Auburn Trust Company.

This is the funeral procession of the first Auburn veteran killed in World War I. The wagon, carrying the body of Alden M. Gayton, is flanked by Army personnel. American Legion Post 31 is named after this brave soldier.

A local Civil War company on the field was captured in this early photograph.

The Auburn Drum Corp., as seen on the Auburn side of the Androscoggin River with the falls in the background.

These five Civil War veterans have nine legs and six arms between them. From left to right are: (front row) Fred Bumpus and Francis Allen; (standing) unknown, Joseph Durand, and S.F. Haskell.

Three

Residences

The Davis sisters, who taught school in Auburn, at one time operated a millinery shop out of their home. The building was later used as the Legion Hall, and then as a municipal building. It was eventually torn down and the Auburn Theatre was built on the site. The theatre was torn down in 1961 and replaced by a parking lot.

This building, located at 7 Cushman Place (or 235 Minot Avenue), was once owned by Ara Cushman, founder of the Cushman-Hollis Shoe Factory.

The foundation is being laid for the home at the corner of Elm and Main Streets. Between 1913 and 1963 various members of the family of Dr. Walter J. Pennell owned the residence, including his wife Leila F. Pennell and his daughters Florence and Edith. The house on the right was a two-family house owned by Dr. Prebles; the house on the left, hidden by tress, had six apartments, and was owned by Mrs. Ryerson.

The old Perkins farmhouse was located on Perkins Ridge, which overlooks Lake Auburn and Taylor Pond. Perkins Ridge was named for Deacon James Perkins, who owned all the land on the ridge and had a blacksmith shop at the north end of the ridge near a brook. Deacon Perkins was a deacon at the East Auburn Church, and he donated land for the cemetery.

The Sturgis home was located on Beech Hill Road, in the Danville area of Auburn.

Squire Andrew Giddings' home was located in Danville, in the early days of Auburn. Squire Giddings was a close friend of Squire Edward Little.

This photograph of Highland Avenue was taken about 1883. The home in the background on the left was the J.C. Symes residence; the home in the foreground is the Charles Gay residence.

This residence, located on the corner of Main and Drummond Streets, was the birthplace of the long-time *Lewiston Journal* sports editor, Norman S. Thomas Sr.

This is the interior of the home where Norman S. Thomas Sr. was born on January 12, 1893.

The formal dining room in the Waites' residence, located at 429 Maine Street in Lewiston, was photographed around 1900. David S. Waites, of the Bates Street Shirt Company, was a major employer in both Auburn and Lewiston.

The old Elm House was originally built in 1830 on Court Street for Josiah Little. In 1836 it changed hands, and in 1845 it became a public stagecoach tavern. This photograph was taken in 1891. The Elm House was named for the great elm trees lining the street.

This home, very similar in style and age to the Thomas birthplace, was also located on Drummond Street.

This interior view shows an example of home decor in the 1890s.

Four

Schools and Games

The Washburn School was first built on a lot at Whitney Street and Lake Auburn Avenue in 1892. Additions were made in 1950 and 1953.

This is a 1905–1906 photograph of the Edward Little High School Glee Club. From left to right are: (front row) unknown, Carl Stevens, Clinton Bonney, and Merton Vining; (middle row) Harry Atwood, unknown, Peter Lawton, Claude Bower, Professor Condon, Frank Haskell, unknown, and John E. Libby; (back row) Stanley Attwood, George Bray, Clyde Merrill, unknown, Chester White, Hale Sawtell, Arthur Pratt, Albert Aug?, and Charles Adams.

These students attended the Park Hill School in the 1890s. From front to back are: (far left row) Arthur Shaw, John Littlefield, Lloyd McFadden, Fannie Bennett, Alice Bennett, and teacher Grace Ingersoll; (middle row) Gladys Chapman, Annie Woodbury, Gladys Woodman, Ralph Olfene, Hazel Keene, and Charles Harradon; (far right row) Arthur Whitehouse, Fred Littlefield, Harry Goss, Grace Lunt, Laura Knight, Henry Bennett, and Will Bennett.

This Washburn School classroom was photographed in 1895 or 1896. Included in this image are: teachers Ida Smith, Lena Packard, Miss Cummings (later Mrs. H. Bumpus), and Miss Pinkham (all standing at the rear of the room, from left to right); Lucinda Loring (the little girl standing); Martha Bekler (the little girl in the third seat behind Lucinda, with the dark, white-ruffled dress); Lona Tarr (the little girl in front of the window in the plaid dress); and Etta Davis (in the front seat at the right).

This photograph of the Franklin School on Pine Street was taken in the spring of 1889 or 1890.

These well-wishers attended the football game between Portland and Edward Little High School in 1897.

The Free-will Baptist Church was located on Marston Corner in the Danville area of Auburn. The original church was erected in 1841 and dedicated on May 11, 1842. Jonathan Tracy was the pastor at the time. Over the years, the following additions have been made: the galley in 1852; the vestry in 1927; the belfry in 1932; and the steeple in 1955.

This is a view of the Danville Corner School, with students and teachers arranged in front.

The Edward Little High School football team posed for this photograph in 1924. The young man holding the football is Howard Thomas; the "manager" on the right is Harry Schulman.

This team was the Edward Little High School Basketball Champions of 1918–1919.

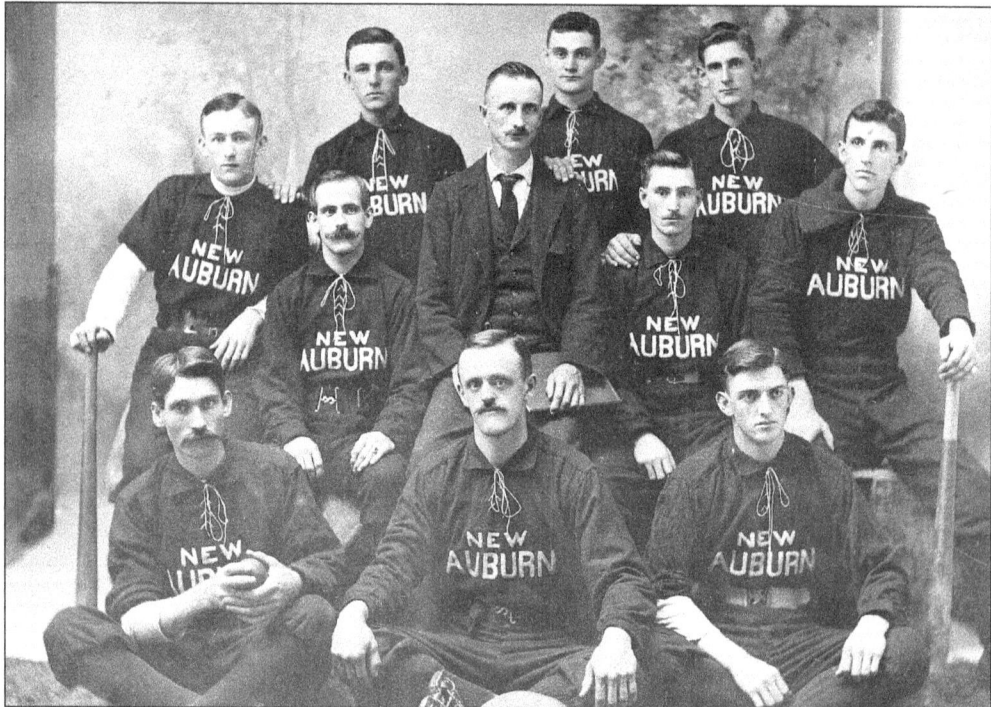

The new Auburn B.B.C. paused for a photograph during the 1894 season. From left to right are: (front row) Spearrin, Merrow, and Pulsifer; (middle row) Casey, Henry Nason, Bean, Hartwell, and Penley; (back row) Martin, Leonard, and "Hod" Nason.

The Edward Little Freshman Class of 1911 posed for this photograph, taken during the school year of 1907–1908. From left to right are: (front row) Wallingfrod, Fuller, Pilot, Greenan, Cohen, Berry, Bird, Smith, Hammond, Bailey, Allen, Robinson, Libby, Folsom, Marston, Lyford, Whitney, and Elliot; (second row) Hutchinson, S. Merrill, G. Merrill, James, Blaisdell, Beals, Lelansky, Miller, Payson, Norris, Pratt, Luce, Woodbury, Urnship, Maycomber, and Foss; (third row) Everett, Harding, Goddard, Greenleaf, Hatch, Hamilton, Rounds, Hendrikson, Thortin, Cooper, Bunker, Shaw, Stone, Strout, Helen, Marr, and Davis; (fourth row) Dunn, Bonney, Chapman, Collins, Beane, Wilker, James, Given, Alden, Mink, Cobb, Greenleaf, Grey, Gowell, MacFadden, Merrow, Skinner, and Bassett; (back row) Records, Brown, Eugley, Towle, Beals, Tebbets, Tarr, Francis, Magrath, Gordon, March, Smith, Merrill, Mason, Love, Gilbert, and Seavey. Everett, Webber, Pelletier, and Turgeon were not photographed.

This is the Edward Little High School Orchestra of 1922–1923. From left to right are: (front row) Marian Skillings, Ena Bolduc, Russell Anderson, Mr. Elbridge Petcher, Arthur Taylor, Harold Dow, Ida Bisbee, and Elizabeth Tighe; (second row) Irma Francis, Hazel Jones, Katherine Johnson, Audrey Estes, unknown, Clayton Taylor, Elaine Stephens, Eva Miller, and Sadie Bornstein?; (third row) Rae Spaulding, Alden Getchell, Ann Tighe, Sylvia Hoit, Evelyn Chandler, and Francis McCarthy; (fourth row) Lydia Howard, Gerald Newman, Doris Fitz, Wyland Leadbetter, Charlie Jordan, and Charles Siegal; (fifth row) Henry White, Elwyn Gamage, Helen Merrill, and Archer Jordan.

This is the cast of the senior drama, *The Middle Path*, written by Kenneth Ames and Erwin Canharm, who were members of the senior class. From left to right are: (front row) Lois Simpson, Dana Fogg, Crystal Hasley, Florence Pennell Gremley, Daniel Shanahan, and Ina Shannon Read; (back row) Wendall Clark, Joseph Shapiro, Everett Libby, Clyde McKenney, Sara Cann, Kenneth Conner, and Rupert Packard.

This photograph, probably taken around 1895, shows the Franklin School teachers and "Grandpa Davis." Included in this image are: (front row) Etta Bearce, a widow with three sons (Winfield, Edwin, and George, all graduates of Edward Little High School and the University of Maine); and Principal Sarah E. Ingersoll, who taught at the Franklin School for over fifty years and was selected by the federal government to operate a model school at the Jamestown Exposition in 1907; (back row) Ida Smith, who at one time was the "drawing" teacher; "physical culture" teacher Carrie Peables; and William H. Davis, a janitor who lived at 29 Western Promenade, and at one time may have lived in the Danville area of Auburn.

On June 1, 1910, these students of the Washburn School posed for a photographer. From left to right are: (front row) Arthur Reynolds, Irving Chittick, unknown, unknown, Christopher Dean, Albert Gowell, Raymond Fitz, and unknown; (middle row) Selvin McGillvery, Dorothy Sawyer, Teddy S., Mirrian Faxion, Alberta King, Hazel Winthrop, unknown, and H. Marshall; (back row) Louisa Butterfield, Annie Condon, Hattie Holman, Lucille Goss, Beatrice Pulsifer, Laura Timberlake, and Agnes Reynolds.

Miss Brown was a teacher at the Washburn School when this class photograph was taken in 1914. Included in this image are: Dorothy Sawyer, Hazel Jones, Dorothy Wellman, Lucille Goss, Marvin Faxon, Inkaborg Avenenson, Harold Verrill, Pearly Woodman, Beryl Butterfield, Gwendolin Blagdon, Loreda Butterfield, Grace Penley, Florence Farrah, Helen Cronin, Alberta Niles, Hazel Wentworth, Hazel Philbrook, Ruth Huston, Irene Hall, Clement Small, John Marshall, William Bridge, Harold Corey, Isabel Allen, Olive Norris, Dorothy Simpson, Geneva Buckley, Beatrice Pulsifer, Eleanor Stevens, Ruth Lewis, Eleanor Litchfield, Harlan Bumpus, Ralph Hann, Omar Bean, Elmer Darling, Ralph Blagdon, Sandy Rowe, Raymond Fitz, Donald Fogg, Lawrence Bridge, Arthur Robinson, Irving Chittick, John Hooper, Lester Whitney, Hazen Jewett, George Osgood, Leo Flannigan, and Lelwin McGilvany.

Students of Littlefield's Corner School were photographed in 1892. From left to right are: (front row) Lizzie Small, Lillian Martin, Lenora A. Merrow, Belle Cary, Lillian Talcott, Beryl Stevens, Elsie Merrow, ? Talcott, Eva Gore (on steps), Ethel Andrews, Herbert Pettingil (on steps), Clarence Strout, Percy Strout, Harry Strout, Charles Pettingill, Dodd Randall, Bert Gore, Eugene Martin, and Lester S. M?; (back row) Lottie Martin, Lola Martin, Grace Merrow, Stell Martin, Delbert Andrews, Cyrus Flagg, teacher Eva M. Libby, John C. McKenney, Edward Flagg, Fred L. Martin, Harry Stevens, ? B. Merrow, and Lewellyn Small.

The Literary Society of Edward Little High School posed for this 1927 photograph. From left to right are: (front row) Gene Fosdich, Harrison Greenleaf, Phineas Foodkowsky, Lawrence Parker, and Katherine Stetson; (middle row) Helen Shapio, Leonard Allen, Florence Pennell, Wendell Roy, Elizabeth Sawyer, and Evelyn Huntley; (back row) Muene Wiaber, Alice Sawtell, Edith Pennell, Grace Hodgkins, and Betty Mann.

These students attended the Franklin School in 1909. From left to right are: (front row) Byron Wood, Marguerite Lovett, Doris ?, Elsie ?, Evelyn Brown, Mable Cole, Eleanor Stevens, and Bernard Wood; (second row) Merton Spiller, Verna ?, Helen MacFarland, Madeline Milliken, Florence Adams, Caroline Cushman, and Lila ?; (third row) Clinton Sturtevant, Dorothy Billings, Catherine Murphy, Eleanor ?, Ethel Manning, Charlotte Hunt, and unknown; (fourth row) unknown, Richard ?, Ralph (Gatchell or Bennett), Alton ?, Milton Lyon, and the teacher, Miss Curtis; (back row) Kenneth Filed, Arthur (Neale?), unknown, Clifford ?, Maurice Davis, and Maurice Snell.

This photograph of students at the Edward Little High School was taken in 1889. Prominent members of this graduating class include some of the following: Mrs. Helen Roxbury, a noted composer of music; Dr. Wallace E. Webber of Lewiston, a well-known physician; Major George C. Webber, a leading attorney; Dr. Archer Jordan of Auburn, a notable dentist; Mrs. Florence Stinchfield, a studied "voice" abroad; and Ernest Weed, the class valedictorian who became a Portland druggist.

This is a 1907 photograph of the Edward Little High School Oracle Bard. From left to right are: (front row) Ruth Sweetser and Hazel Barnard; (middle row) Clara Butler, Mellen Pingree, Elizabeth Ingersoll, Edward Smith, and Helen Pingree; (back row) Charles Adams, Irma Stevens, John E. Libby, Jessie Alley, Russell Smith, and Grace Connor.

Five

Manufacturers and Proprietors

This is the "cookie crew" at the T.H. Huston cracker factory, in a photograph taken on October 16, 1908.

Crates of oranges, ready for delivery at the Johnson and Kimball Store on North Main Street, are shown here being unloaded at the Grand Trunk Railroad Depot warehouse.

The Fred McKenney filling station, located at the corner of Court and Goff Streets, was one of the first filling stations in the area.

Jonas Edwards and his team are shown here in 1896. Mr. Edwards was an importer of horses and dealt in harnesses and carriages. He operated his place of business at the corner of Union and Hampshire Streets, in Auburn.

Johnson & Kimball, located at 46 North Main Street, was a purveyor of wholesale produce. The business later moved to Turner and Pleasant Streets, and then moved again to Hampshire Street and became the G.B. Johnson Company.

At one time, the Auburn Savings Bank and the First National Bank operated and shared the same quarters on Main Street. From left to right are: Horace Day, the treasurer of the First National Bank; Leslie Lord, a teller of the First National Bank; Deacon George H. Brown, the treasurer of the Auburn Savings Bank; and Bernard Chase, a clerk of the Auburn Savings Bank.

Cyrus R. Kimball's business was located on Knight Street.

I.C. Lombard's shoe shop was located on Goff Hill about 1864. Mr. Lombard began his shoe shop as a small operation in 1852. At the time of this photograph he employed approximately one hundred people.

Employees of the Lunn and Sweet Shoe Company line up with their Christmas holiday gift baskets, complete with turkey and all the fixings.

These foremen and salesmen of the Lunn and Sweet Shoe Company were photographed on February 7, 1913, in Auburn. From left to right are: (front row) Walter Holmes and William Cliff; (middle row) Charles Ault and Timothy O'Leary; (back row) A.J. Sweet and Ralph Lunn.

The office of the Lunn and Sweet Shoe Company was photographed in the early part of this century. The woman in the foreground is Hazel Snow, and the two men seated behind her are Charles Ault (left) and Walter Holmes (right). The three women standing on the right side of the room are, from left to right: Mary Keith, Pauline Whitney, and Ethel Jackson. Other women in the room are believed to be Marguerite Snow, Carrie Gordon, Edna Woodward, Ruby Hutchinson, Winifred Hackett, Daisy Francis, Marion Meek, and Helen Linehan.

This is the Foss Packard Shoe Company as it appeared in the late 1800s, located on Maine Street in a building that once stood across from the Roak Block and next door to the Maine Hotel. The factory was later known as the Maine Shoe Company before it was razed.

Huston's Bakery was located on the shores of the Androscoggin River, just north of the bridge in the present park.

The Auburn Trust Company was located in the "Elm Block" near the corner of Court and Maine Streets, adjacent to what was then the "Oscar Jones" drug store. The Auburn Trust Company closed its doors in 1902, and the real estate was purchased and occupied by the Auburn Savings Bank.

The Knights of Pythias Building, located on Mill Street in New Auburn, burned in the 1933 fire.

The E.N. Palmer Print Shop was located on Court Street.

This photograph of an Auburn Bankers baseball game at Lewiston Park was taken about 1905. From left to right are: (front row) William Greenleaf (National Shoe & Leather Bank) and Bernard Chase (Auburn Savings Bank); (back row) Horace Day (First National Bank, Auburn), Mr. Stetson (Mechanics Savings Bank), Linwood E. Ashton (First National Bank), Chester Miller (First National Bank), Wesley Day (First National Bank), Wills Atwood (National Shoe & Leather Bank), and R.E. Smith (National Shoe & Leather Bank).

The first Dillingham and Sons Funeral Parlor was located next to the Auburn Fire Station.

The E.W. Penley Plant, a meat-packing business, was located at 37 Knight Street. Captain John Penley, an early resident of the Danville area of Auburn, originally bought beef and cattle and drove them to the Brighton market in Massachusetts. Captain Penley's son Fernidad set up a butchering plant on the Durham/Auburn Road in South Auburn in 1865. He later purchased a small slaughterhouse from Nathaniel Knight on Knight Street. In 1900, Fernidad sold the business to his son Eugene, who expanded the business that produced Penley's famous "Blue Tag Brand" hams, bacon, and sausage.

Six

Gettin' Around

One of the first oil-delivery trucks in the area, owned by Fred McKenny, was photographed under the Turner Street underpass.

Fred Wright is shown here with his "cow-drawn" wagon in the early 1880s.

"Old Don" and this carriage were owned by C.A. Kimball of 158 Gamage Avenue.

The Lewiston-Auburn Airport had its beginnings in 1933 on 340 acres of leased land in the Marston Corner area of Auburn. Henry M. Dingley Jr., an early aviation buff, leased the early operation of the airport in 1936, and promoted the paving and lighting of runways. This photograph depicts the new hanger on the old Hotel Road side of the airport, built by the WPA in 1939. The airplane on the left is a WACO cabin bi-plane owned by Henry Dingley. The airplane on the right is a Piper "J-3" Cub.

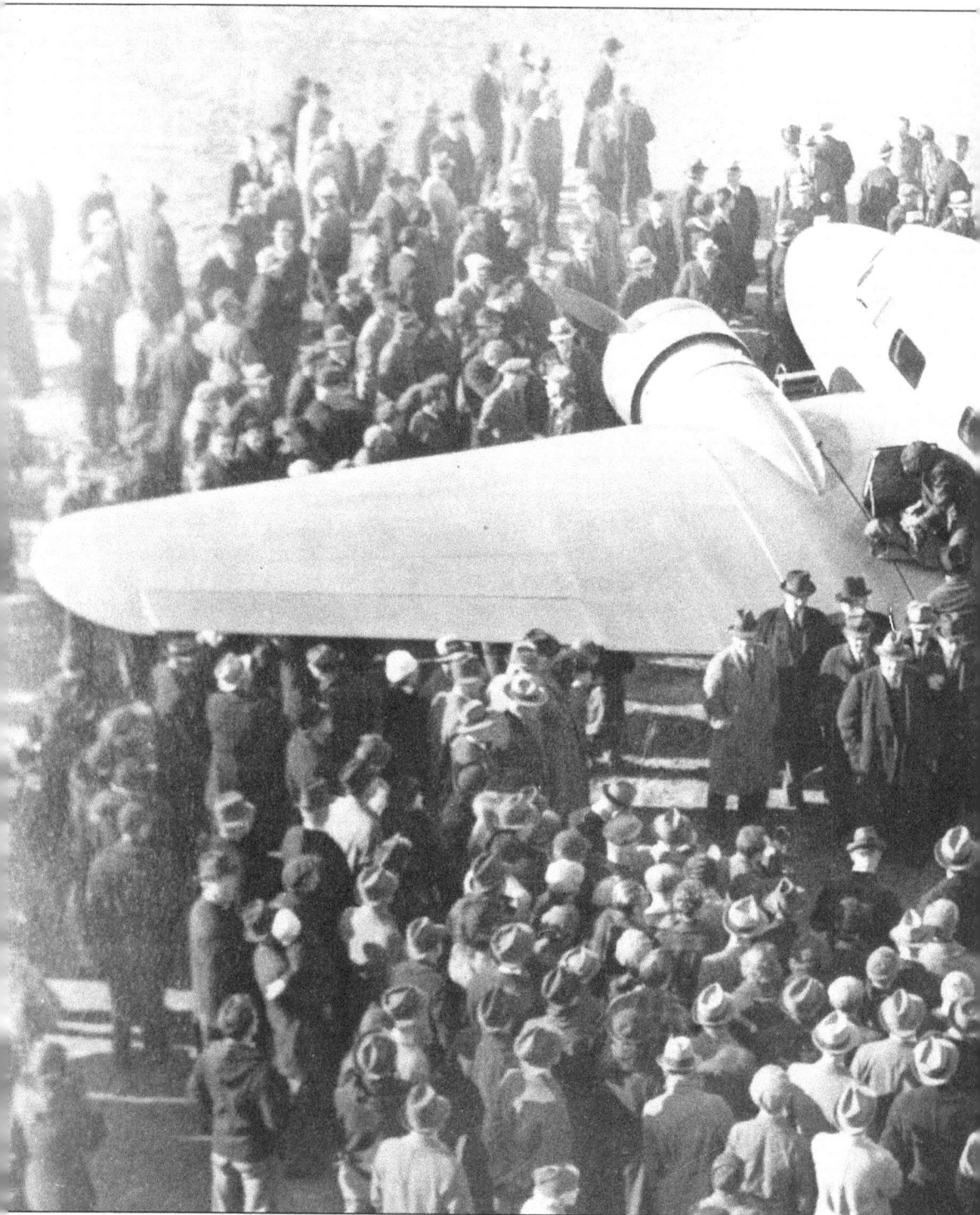

In June 1938 the new Boston and Maine Airway Lockheed L-10 made a promotional relations visit to the Lewiston-Auburn Airport. This airplane is similar to the one flown by Amelia Earhart on her last flight in an attempt to circle the globe. By 1940, Boston and Maine airplanes

were making scheduled flights to the Lewiston-Auburn Airport. Boston and Maine Airways later became Northeast Airlines, which in turn was acquired by Delta Airlines in 1972.

This is the Danville Junction Railroad Station.

This four-seat platform wagon was an early example of transportation before the invention of the "horseless carriage."

This boy and his St. Bernard are ready for an outing.

Seven

Street Scenes

This horse and carriage was photographed at the corner of Court and Turner Streets while out for a stroll.

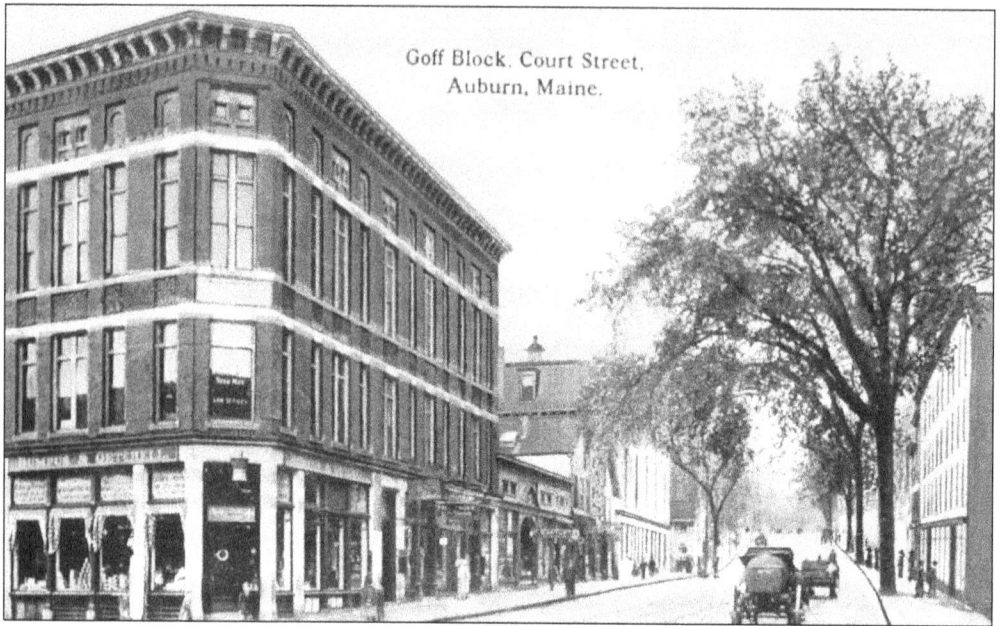

At the turn of the century, tenants of the Goff Block on Court Street included "Bumpus and Getchell," "Seth May Law Offices," and "Fred L. Robie Clothing."

This postcard view shows some of the shops located on Maine Street.

This photograph of Court Street was taken about 1924.

Court Street is shown here in another postcard view.

The beautiful Lake Grove House was located in East Auburn.

Libby's Bakery was located on the corner of Court and Turner Streets.

This scenic view was taken from Edward Little High School.

A somber Dingley Funeral procession was captured on film by an onlooker.

Court Street is shown here in the early 1890s.

In this early scene of Court Street, note the giant Elm tree, with its branches and boughs spreading over the street. The Elm House is behind the tree.

The Shapiro Block, at the corner of Mill and Broad Streets in the early 1900s, was later destroyed during the big fire of 1933. Barker Mill is in the background to the right.

The Auburn Library, built in 1903, is still in use at the present. Previous to 1903, the library was located with the Auburn Trust Company on Court Street next to the Elm House, and in 1899 it was located in the American Legion Home, which was also the city building at that time.

Ted Maguire is shown here pushing the refuse street cart at the corner of Court and Main Streets. Note the neon sign for the electric company and the trolley tracks in the foreground.

The Ruggles Block, located at the corner of Turner and Summer Streets, is shown here in a turn-of-the-century photograph.

This is the northeast corner of Court and Main Streets; note the grooved trolley tracks that run down the middle of the street. In the foreground, Samuel B. Smith, hatter, advertised his wares by the means of an oversized "top" hat on a pole in front of his shop. Fred C. Mower operated a clothing store above the hatter, and there was a druggist located across the street that advertised with signs for "trusses, crutches, and supports."

The Seth May family home at 9 Laurel Avenue was photographed at the turn of the century. Mr. May was a prominent lawyer in the early 1900s and became an Auburn city solicitor in 1912. He was also a Federal Prohibition director for twelve years and was instrumental in prosecuting pollution cases that lead to the cleanup of the Androscoggin River in the 1940s. He passed away in 1959 at the age of seventy-four.

This view from the road shows the east end of the "Old Peg Shop" in East Auburn. The man standing at the window is Mr. Waterman; the man outside is Mr. Alanson Berry, who rebuilt the dam for Lockwood and French. The man at the door of the gatehouse is "Uncle Erskins," who was "Jim Clark's boss."

Bobbin Mill Brook, which flows from Lake Auburn into the Androscoggin River, is shown here with the Old Given Farm in the background.

The George Jones residence was located on Goff Street in 1886, before the development of James Street.

This is a view of the corner of Court and Turner Streets, as Turner Street enters on the left. Note the trolley car crossing the North Bridge in the distance.

The East Auburn Bobbin Mill, powered by steam, was located in the area of the outlet by Oak Hill Road.

The George E. Wills Jewelry Store was located on Court Street. It is not known if Mr. Wills is in the photograph; if so, the photograph was taken prior to his death in 1925.

This is a view of the Webster School, encircled by trees.

Maine Street, complete with a horse-drawn trolley, is shown here in the early 1890s, near the intersection with Elm Street.

Eight

The Androscoggin, Lake Auburn, and Other Waterways

This is an early 1890s photograph of Lake Grove on Lake Auburn.

The steamer *Lewiston* plied the waters of Lake Auburn for many years.

This view of Taylor Brook was taken in 1918.

Jacobs Stevens, originally from Gloucester, Massachusetts, settled in Auburn in 1789, on "Lot 97," which consisting of 500 acres. His two children, Moses and Parker, built this sawmill on Taylor Brook in 1800. The mill continued in operation until 1860.

Brook trout were hatched and raised at the fish hatchery, on the Lumber Mill Road, off the Turner Road. The fish hatchery closed in the early 1960s.

This photograph of the impressive Lake Auburn Spring House was taken sometime between its construction in 1889 and January 30, 1893, when it was destroyed by fire.

F.R. Whitney was the captain of the steamer *Lewiston* from 1885 to 1886. J. Owen Jr. took this photograph of the steamer on the shores of Lake Auburn.

The Flood of 1896, which began after a heavy rainstorm at the end of February and beginning of March, washed away the two bridges connecting Auburn and Lewiston. This photograph below shows the Old North Bridge, before it was washed away in the flood.

The South Bridge is shown here before the Flood of 1896. Note the wooden supports used on this bridge and the teams of horses pulling the sleighs.

The South Ferry, established after the Flood of 1896, provided temporary ferry service between the twin cites after the bridges were washed away during the flood. The stone piers of the South Bridge can be seen in the distance.

The "Grandview," also known as the Eastern Star House, was located diagonally across from the James Munroe home on Spring Road. The original hotel opened in 1880, and became the "Grandview" in 1882, under the management of S.E. Brown. Many also called the establishment the "sanatorium," because of the clear fresh water it served its patrons. Businessmen from Boston purchased the hotel in 1905 along with a strip of land along Lake Auburn, hoping to draw a large tourist trade. The hotel subsequently failed, and closed it in 1908. It later became a "rest home" and was torn down in 1918.

The Lake Auburn Spring House was not a success as a hotel, and became insolvent. Eventually its only occupant was the caretaker. It burned on January 30, 1893.

The Lake Auburn Spring House is shown here under construction in 1889, on the shores of Lake Auburn. The original venture consisted of a small hotel, established by the Lake Auburn Mineral Spring Company. The Lake Auburn steamer, the *Lewiston*, docked at its wharf. The Spring House offered its guests spring water, and it bottled ginger ale, sarsaparilla, and soda for sale.

Horace Edward Munroe, John Merrill, and John Cartwright survey the scene at the corner of Court and Main Streets during the Flood of 1936.

Miller Street in Auburn is shown here during the Flood of 1896.

The first horse-drawn streetcar, which carried passengers from Auburn to Lake Grove, was chartered in 1881, and is shown here in 1886 at the corner of Court and Goff Streets. Its driver, Mr. Fred Bird of Auburn, operated the streetcar year-round for ten years, on the tracks in the summer months and on runners in the winter, even in the most inclement weather. The Lake Grove line ran to the East Auburn Theatre, the Dance Hall, and the Steamer line.

The Maine Central Railroad Bridge and the Island Garden Bridge, a suspension bridge, crossed the Androscoggin River. Island Garden, a small island in Lewiston, located just above the Lewiston Falls, was the site of a new amusement park, considered by some to be the "Coney Island" of Lewiston/Auburn. The island was developed at a cost of $10,000 by Frank W. Dana of Lewiston, and initially consisted of a pavilion, shaded walkways, a fish pond, booths, and attractive landscaping.

Construction is shown here of the water lines above Lewiston Falls on the Androscoggin River.

In the winter of 1913, ice was cut and harvested on the Androscoggin River using horse-drawn plows. Gas-powered saws later replaced the plows. The Auburn Crystal Ice Company, a local firm, cut ice on the Androscoggin River and Lake Auburn.

Nine

Police, Fire, and Politics

In 1910 these horse-drawn fire engines lined up in front of the Engine House for a photograph.

This is a c. 1950s photograph of an Auburn Fire Department truck.

Auburn Fire Department Engine #6 is shown here in front of the "Jenny" gas station.

The Civil War Memorial Statue can be seen in this view of the Androscoggin County Courthouse.

The Auburn Fire Department posed at the "Muster" at Bath in 1898.

In 1882 the Civil War Memorial Statue was erected by Auburn citizens, in front of the Androscoggin County Courthouse, in memory of "Her Noble Sons."

The Auburn Fire Department races by the library and passes a trolley car in response to an alarm.

This is a 1932 photograph of the Auburn Police Department. From left to right are: (front row) Jerry Boisvert, Sam Ratcliff, Harry Rowe, Joe Shannon, and Henry Parker; (middle row) Frank Davidson, John Staples, Robert Herrick, Mr. Alfred Segendre, A. Patterson, and Joseph Brown; (back row) Edward McCarty, Clarence McIntoch, David Berry, George Moore, and Lawrence Joube.

This is the funeral of George "Pa" Whitney, who drove the horse-drawn ladder truck for the Auburn Fire Department from 1909 to 1919, with Hose #3 being utilized as the hearse. Mr. Whitney's Turner Street home can be seen in the far left. From left to right are: (seated) Fred Tuttle and Chief Chester Blethen; (on the rear) Carl Spearin, Edgar Finley, and Frank Jackson; (on the side) Carl Allen.

Clearing snow was more laborious in the days before snowblowers and trucks with plows.

"Our Neighbourhood Club" was photographed during an outing at Lake Grove. From left to right are: (front row) three Goss children, Helen Garcelon, Mrs. Cushman, C. Peaslee, Harriet ?, Mrs. Alfred Salls, Mrs. E.J. Garland, Carleton Peals (the child), and Mrs. Oscar Jones; (middle row) Mrs. Abby Peaslee, Mrs. George Wentworth, Mrs. Helen Atwood, Mrs. B.F. Beals, Mrs. A. Goss, unknown, and Mrs. Nora P. Libby; (back row) Mrs. Eugene Goss, unknown, Mrs. Frank L. Beals, Mrs. C.C. Peaslee, Mrs. Henry Hildreth, Mrs. Sweetser, Mrs. Levi Curtis, Mrs. Sherman ?, Mrs. Ida E. Havi, and Ada G. Stevens.

The Auburn Fire Department posed for this photograph during a quiet moment.

The Auburn Fire Department's Engine House is now occupied by Bethel Bankcorp and other small businesses.

These were the in-town carriers for the Auburn Post Office. From left to right are: (front row) unknown, unknown, Miller, Bonney, Quimby, and Morrill; (back row) unknown and Keene.

RFD men stand in front of the Rickard Block on Main Street.

This photograph of the Auburn Fire Department was taken in the fall of 1938, after the two new "white pumpers" had been added to the department. The following individuals have been identified: (near Engine #5) Thomas Maguire and James Lawler; (near Engine #4) Willis Millett, Ralph Draper, Franklin Prescott, Walter Currier, and Alton Morrell; (near Hose #1) George Small and Thomas Chifelle; (seated in Engine #3) Carl Stratton and Walter Sawtell; (on the rear step of Engine #3) John MacDonald, Kenneth Calligan, and Harry Sawyer; (on the ground near Engine #3) Clarence Handy, Harry Fogg, Mayor Gree, and George L. Barnes; (near the chief's car) Councilman ?, City Manager David Walton, and Councilman Bussiere

An early 1890s fire engine parades down Court Street, across from Auburn Hall.

Ray; (on the front of Engine #2) Harlan Procotor, Sumner Elwell, and Guy Stewart; (on the rear of Engine #2) Clarence Penley and Patrick Cullinanae; (on ground near Engine #2) Fred Banks and David Simpson; (on Ladder #1) Carlton Proctor, Samuel Towle, William Cross, and Walter Pottle; (on the ground near Ladder #1) George Cadman; (to the left side of Engine #1 on the ground) Warwick Ward; (on the running board of Engine #1) Elmo Gosselin; (seated in Engine #1) Harold Wright and William Bennett; (on the ride side of Engine #1, from top to bottom) Dewey Stepheson, John Magee, and Dexter Knights.

The Auburn Police were photographed on parade in 1914.

The Auburn Fire Department, photographed while on parade.

The Page Box Factory fire, on Washington Street, was captured in this 1896 photograph.

The Auburn Police show off their finest.

Letter carriers pose in front of the Auburn Post Office in 1887, the year houses were numbered.

This jury at the Androscoggin County Courthouse was composed of people from various areas. Included among those shown here, along with their place of residence, are: Robinson, the foreman (Auburn), Hewey (Lewiston), Knapp (Leeds), Libby (Minot), Larrabee (Lewiston), Lufontain (Lisbon), Perkins (Turner), Harlow (Auburn), Prince (Minot), Welch (Lewiston), Pollard (Livermore), and Mills (Auburn).

The "ladder room" of the Auburn Central Fire Station was the setting for the Twin City Indoor Baseball League banquet. Clockwise, beginning at the lower left, are: Howard Nelson, Fred Whirley, Everett Huntley, Carleton Proctor, Walter Pelletier, William Bennett, and Harold Wright (Auburn residents); Paul McGraw, James Donahue, Leo Levesque, Fred Leclair, Albert Moreau, Percy Maguire, Lewis Jones, Abner Hodgon, Eugene Beaudoin, Linwood Edgecomb, Zepherin Dronin, and Gerald Roy (Lewiston residents). In the background is a table converted in 1927 from a horse-drawn hose wagon, which originally carried a load of hoses and a "deck gun" mounted on the hose bed.

This Auburn Board of Trade outing at Rumford Falls was photographed in 1902.

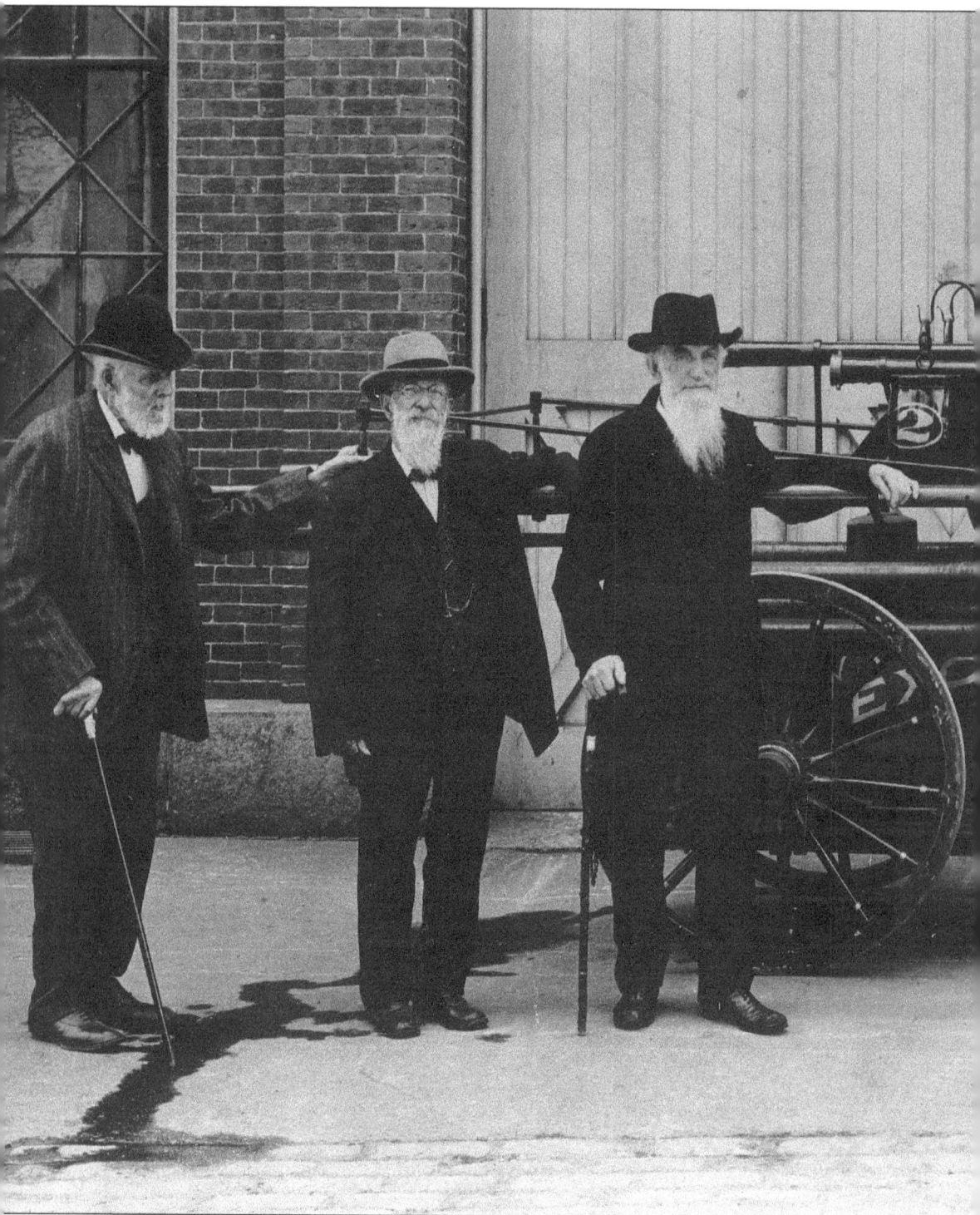

In 1849, two hand pumps were purchased for the Auburn and Lewiston Fire Departments. Lewiston's was named the Androscoggin #1 and Auburn's was named the Excelsior #2. This 1909 photograph depicts prior crew members, as they pose with the Excelsior #2. From left

to right are: Samuel Stetson, age ninety-five; Stephen Hayes, age eighty-two; Seth P. Miller, age eighty-five, was Auburn's mayor for thirty-nine years; Judge Nahum Morrill, age ninety; Captain A.A. Miller, age seventy; and Captain James White, age seventy-eight.

The Androscoggin County Courthouse was located on the corner of Turner and Court Streets.

This band is on parade at the corner of North Maine and Court Streets. Note the Elm House in the background.

These people were the members of the Androscoggin County Grand Jury from 1928 to 1929.

Acknowledgments

I would like to offer large quantities of gratitude to my husband Richard, and my children Erin and Eric, for their patience and understanding as I spent countless hours away from them physically and mentally, researching and compiling the material for this book. I would like to thank my parents, Bud and Carole McLellan, for instilling in me the curiosity and enthusiasm to begin this venture and the determination to complete it. I would like to extend a warm thank you to the area libraries and their employees, who were most generous with their collections and assistance, materials, and time. I could not have completed this book without the ongoing, never-ending help and cheers I received from my friend and mentor, Robert Taylor, Executive Secretary of the Androscoggin County Historical Society. Mr. Taylor is a well-known historian and genealogist and provided me with information, assistance, encouragement, and friendly laughter while doing my research. Finally, I would like to thank the Androscoggin Historical Society for allowing the use of a portion of their photograph collection in this book.

.

www.ingramcontent.com/pod-product-compliance
Lightning Source LLC
Chambersburg PA
CBHW080848100426
42812CB00007B/1963